Federal Tax Benefits for Manufacturing: Current Law, Legislative Proposals, and Issues for the 112th Congress

Gary Guenther
Analyst in Public Finance

September 20, 2012

Congressional Research Service

7-5700
www.crs.gov
R42742

CRS Report for Congress
Prepared for Members and Committees of Congress

Summary

Congress is considering numerous proposals to create new forms of targeted assistance for the manufacturing sector. One of the more contentious issues in the policy debate concerns the role federal policy should play in the allocation of economic resources to and within the sector.

This report examines a key element of current federal support for manufacturing: tax benefits. More specifically, it identifies and describes current federal tax preferences that offer significant benefits for small and large manufacturing firms. To broaden the context for the current policy debate over federal support for manufacturing, the report also provides a brief overview of federal non-tax support for manufacturing. In addition, the report identifies bills in the 112th Congress that would enhance current tax preferences and explains how eligible manufacturers might be affected. It concludes with a discussion of the chief arguments for and against additional targeted support for manufacturing and their implications for federal policy.

Current federal tax law contains nine provisions with a strong potential to provide significant tax relief to firms primarily engaged in manufacturing. A few of them are targeted at manufacturing; the others tend to benefit manufacturers more than firms in most other sectors. The provisions include the deferral of the active income of controlled foreign subsidiaries of U.S.-based corporations, the research tax credit, the expensing of outlays for research and experimentation, and accelerated depreciation for certain capital assets.

Numerous bills have been introduced in the 112th Congress that would enhance some of these tax preferences or create new ones. Among the notable proposals are H.R. 10/S. 1237, H.R. 689, H.R. 1036, H.R. 3476, H.R. 3495, H.R. 5727, S. 256, S. 825, and S. 2237. There is considerable variation among the bills in the extent to which they would benefit manufacturing firms. Several would extend and enhance the research tax credit, extend the generous depreciation allowances that were available in 2011, and allow a full exclusion for gains on small business stock.

Proponents of targeted federal assistance for manufacturing make several arguments to back their stance. First, they say the assistance is needed to help the United States become more dependent on exports and domestic production as sources of economic growth. Second, a federal manufacturing policy, in their view, would encourage the creation of more manufacturing jobs, which pay higher wages and benefits, on average, than do non-manufacturing jobs. Third, proponents point out that manufacturing industries perform the vast share of private-sector research and development, and innovation is a primary engine of economic growth. Fourth, they note that manufacturing plays a critical role in the growth of the green economy. And because many foreign governments provide assistance to their manufacturers, say proponents, the United States should do the same to avoid a loss of competitiveness.

By contrast, critics of special federal assistance for manufacturing say it is not warranted on economic grounds, since there is no discernible market failure that is peculiar to goods production. They also maintain that promoting job growth in manufacturing would do little to create the millions of jobs needed to achieve full employment again. Finally, in their view, the U.S. economy would benefit more from increased efforts by the federal government to dismantle foreign barriers to expanding U.S. exports of services than from policies aimed at boosting the competitiveness of U.S. manufacturers.

Contents

Figures

Tables

Contacts

Introduction

In his State of the Union speech delivered in January 2012, President Obama stated that his strategy for economic recovery and growth "begins with manufacturing.[1]" About two months later, Gene Sperling, the Director of the President's National Economic Council, explained the rationale for this strategy in an address to the Conference on the Renaissance of American Manufacturing.[2] He argued that building a plan to revitalize the economy around manufacturing is justified by the "outsized" role played by the sector in innovation, the creation of high-wage jobs, and exports. Further enhancing the sector's economic importance, according to Sperling, were the spillover benefits of manufacturing for other firms and the communities where manufacturing facilities are located and the significant economic harm associated with a lasting loss of manufacturing production.

Statements such as these have drawn attention to a longstanding debate among lawmakers and some policy analysts over the economic role of manufacturing and whether there is a justifiable need for special federal support for companies primarily engaged in manufacturing activities. In the exchange of views on these issues in the aftermath of the President's speech, a difference of opinion has emerged that is reminiscent of the policy disputes that characterized the debate over industrial policy in the late 1970s and early 1980s. On the one hand, proponents of special government assistance to promote the growth and competitiveness of manufacturing companies argue that the sector deserves such support because it contributes more to the performance and growth of the economy than other sectors do. On the other hand, critics of such assistance maintain that what matters most for promoting increases in jobs, real wages, and output are public investments in the main forces that drive growth in the standard of living: namely, worker skills, public education, research and development (R&D), and economic infrastructure. In their view, sector-based policies are bound to fail because the federal government cannot do a better job than market forces in identifying the industries that will grow rapidly in the future and generate large numbers of well-paying jobs.

The ongoing debate over whether the manufacturing sector deserves targeted government assistance continues in the 112th Congress. Numerous bills have been introduced to provide new or enhanced federal support for manufacturing companies. Some of the proposals would do so by using tax preferences to bolster their competitiveness and encourage increased domestic production and job creation in manufacturing. These initiatives are attracting attention at a time when Congress is considering options for reforming the federal tax system as a key element of a broader plan to eliminate or substantially lower projected federal budget deficits. To critics of the current federal income tax, proposals for new or enhanced tax benefits for manufacturing underscore what they regard as a critical problem with the system: it is laden with special benefits that reduce effective tax rates and act in the same manner as federal spending, except that the spending is not subject to the scrutiny and oversight built into the appropriations and authorization processes.

---

[1] See http://www.whitehouse.gov/the-press-office/2012/01/24/remarks-president-state-union-address.

[2] For a text of the speech, see http://www.whitehouse.gov/sites/default/files/administration-official/sperling_-_renaissance_of_american_manufacturing_-_03_27_12.pdf.

To provide helpful background information for the congressional debate over whether manufacturing deserves targeted federal support, this report addresses a key component of that support: tax benefits.[3] More specifically, it summarizes the main federal tax preferences under current law from which manufacturing firms derive significant benefits, identifies the bills in the 112th Congress that would enhance those preferences benefits and how they would affect manufacturers, and discusses the arguments for and against additional targeted support for the manufacturing sector and their implications for federal policy. To broaden the context for the current policy debate over federal support for manufacturing, the report also provides a brief overview of federal non-tax support for manufacturing. It will be updated as warranted by changes in tax law or congressional action.

Manufacturing and the U.S. Economy

According to the North American Industrial Classification System (NAICS), the manufacturing sector is composed of establishments that are primarily engaged in the transformation of materials, substances, or components into new products.[4] Establishments in this case consist of factories, plants, or mills that use power-driven machines and equipment in the transformation process. But they also include individuals who transform materials, substances, and components into products by hand in their homes and small businesses that sell directly to the public items they make on their premises.

Products made by manufacturing establishments may be finished or semi-finished. The former are ready for consumption or final use, while the latter serve as inputs for the production of finished products. For the sake of national income accounting and the collection of detailed economic data, the manufacturing sector is broken down into a variety of sub-sectors (or industries) that reflect three critical aspects of the production process: material inputs, machinery and equipment, and employee skills. The output of some industries becomes the input of others, and vice versa. For example, makers of machine tools buy many needed materials and components directly from the producers of these items, while the latter purchase machine tools directly from the former for use in the production of the materials and components.

Still, the boundaries between manufacturing and other sectors are blurred in some cases. The uncertainty largely arises from the definition of a new product, which can be subjective. For example, the bottling and processing of milk and spring-fed water are considered manufacturing

---

[3] Federal support for manufacturing is spread among several agencies and lacks centralized control and coordination. The Department of Defense funds research on new product and process technologies through its Manufacturing Technologies Program and the Defense Advanced Research Projects Agency. Under its Industrial Technologies Program, the Department of Energy enters into partnerships with industries to improve their energy efficiency through the development of new process technologies. The National Institute for Standards and Technology (NIST) devotes about half of its annual budget to promoting improved competitiveness among small and medium-sized manufacturing companies through two programs: the Manufacturing Extension Partnership and the Engineering Laboratory. NIST also supports research in advanced manufacturing technologies through the Advanced Manufacturing Technology Consortia Program and the NIST Centers of Excellence program. In addition, the Obama Administration is proposing that Congress appropriate $1 billion through the NIST budget for a competitive grant program to establish a network of regional institutes for manufacturing innovation. In addition, the National Science Foundation funds a significant share of the federally supported basic research done at American colleges and universities. Some of the research funded by NSF has applications in manufacturing; those funds are distributed largely through the Directorate for Engineering's Civil, Mechanical, and Manufacturing Innovation Organization.

[4] See http://www.census.gov/cgi-bin/sssd/naics/naicsrch?code=31&search=2012 NAICS Search.

---

activities, though they involve no transformation of materials or components into new products, whereas the erection of buildings (including the fabrication performed at construction sites) is considered a construction activity.

Manufacturing's role in the U.S. economy has changed considerably since 1960. Back then, it accounted for 27% of gross domestic product (GDP), 31% of non-agricultural employment, more than 20% of domestic non-residential fixed investment, nearly 99% of business investment in research and development (R&D), and 62% of exports. Since the 1970s, however, its contributions to GDP and employment in particular have declined.

The extent of this shift is sketched using several economic indicators in **Figure 1**. Basically, it traces the manufacturing sector's share of non-agricultural employment, gross domestic product (GDP), business investment in research and development (R&D), exports, and domestic investment in capital assets between 1960 and 2010. There was a decline in some measures of importance. Specifically, manufacturing's share of exports in 2010 was down 17% from its level 1960; its share of business R&D investment was 29% smaller; and its contribution to non-agricultural employment decreased by 71%. With the exception of non-agricultural employment, manufacturing's share fell because the total contributions of other sectors rose faster than those of manufacturing. In the case of employment, manufacturing's contribution declined because it lost workers while combined employment in other sectors grew, except during recessions.

Every indicator depicted in **Figure 1** trended downward except one: employee wages and salaries. Labor compensation per employee in manufacturing was somewhat larger in 1960 than it was in most other sectors; the difference grew steadily until the mid-1990s; and in 2010, the gap was 7% smaller than it was in 1995 but nearly 18% larger than it was in 1960. Wages and benefits were consistently higher than manufacturing in several other sectors (e.g., construction, mining, transportation, and utilities) from 1960 to 2010.

What the figure does not show, however, is several related and significant secular trends. First, among all sectors, manufacturing held the largest share of GDP until 1986, when the government sector contributed more to overall output of goods and services (measured in current dollars). Several other sectors have risen in importance since then, and by 2010, government; finance, insurance, real estate, rental and leasing; and professional and business services held larger shares than manufacturing. Second, manufacturing had the largest share of non-agricultural employment among all sectors until 1989, when the government sector employed more persons. Since then, retail trade, professional and business services, education and health services, and leisure and hospitality have joined government as larger employers than manufacturing. Finally, although payroll employment in manufacturing has fallen gradually since 1979, when it reached an all-time peak of 17.985 million, the sector's value added (in current dollars), which is a measure of its contribution to GDP, grew by a factor of 11.9 from 1960 to 2010, when it reached an all-time peak of $1.702 trillion. These contrasting trends underscore the relatively robust growth in productivity within the manufacturing sector over that period. From 1988 to 2010, output per hour of labor rose at an average annual rate of 3.5% in manufacturing, compared to a rate of 2.2% for all non-farm businesses, including manufacturing.

Figure 1. Key Economic Indicators for Manufacturing, 1960 to 2010

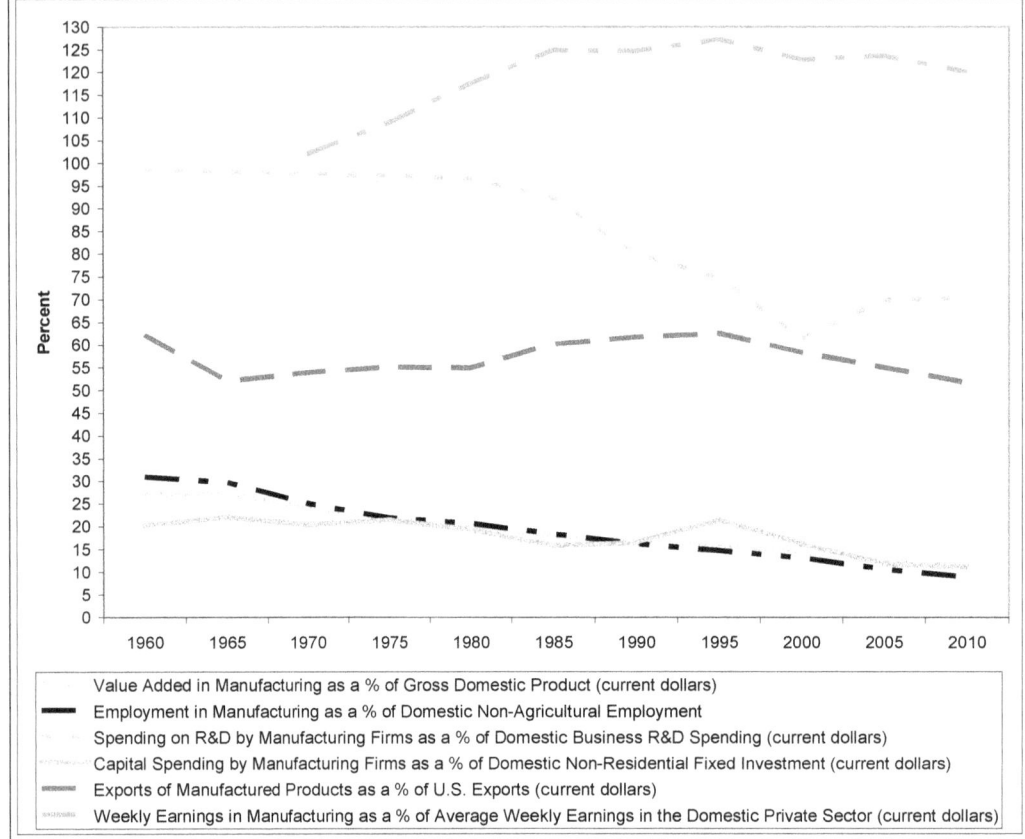

Value Added in Manufacturing as a % of Gross Domestic Product (current dollars)

Employment in Manufacturing as a % of Domestic Non-Agricultural Employment

Spending on R&D by Manufacturing Firms as a % of Domestic Business R&D Spending (current dollars)

Capital Spending by Manufacturing Firms as a % of Domestic Non-Residential Fixed Investment (current dollars)

Exports of Manufactured Products as a % of U.S. Exports (current dollars)

Weekly Earnings in Manufacturing as a % of Average Weekly Earnings in the Domestic Private Sector (current dollars)

Source: Congressional Research Service using data obtained from the Department of Commerce, the Department of Labor, and the National Science Foundation

Figure 1 also masks the diversity in the outcomes among manufacturing firms from 1960 to 2010. Depending on how the manufacturing sector is divided into sub-groups, many different industries could be identified and analyzed. Under the NAICS, which federal agencies use to report industry data, manufacturing consists of durable goods industries and non-durable goods industries, and they in turn are further divided into 10 major industries. The performance of these 20 industries can be evaluated using the same indicators of economic importance shown in the figure.

A comparison of the change in full-time-equivalent (FTE) employment and real value added from 1998 to 2010 suggests that some major industries grew in importance or declined more than others.[5] As the figures in **Table 1** show, FTE employment fell in all the industries, but the extent of the decrease ranged from -9% for food, beverages, and tobacco products to -74.5% for apparel, leather, and similar products. A wider and more diversified range of results comes into view when the focus shifts to industry value added. The 20 industries were evenly split between those whose

---

[5] The comparison does not stretch back before 1998 because that is the first year for which the Bureau of Economic Analysis at the Commerce Department provided an estimate of FTE employment by industry.

real value added increased and those whose real value added decreased from 1998 to 2010. Among those whose contribution to GDP shrank, the decreases ranged from -9% for plastics and rubber products to -46% for apparel, leather, and similar products and -47% for textile mills and products. Among the industries whose contributions to GDP expanded, the increases ranged from 4% for electrical equipment, appliances, and components to a whopping 10,900% for computers and electronic products.

Table 1. Percentage Change in Full-Time-Equivalent (FTE) Employment and Real Value Added[a] for Major U.S. Manufacturing Industries, 1998 to 2010

	Change in FTE Employment	Change in Real Value Added
Manufacturing	-35%	29.5%
Durable Goods Production	-36%	54%
Wood Products	-44%	-8%
Non-Metallic Mineral Products	-33%	-31%
Primary Metals	-45%	-34%
Fabricated Metal Products	-18%	-16%
Machinery	-34%	7%
Computers and Electronic Products	-40%	10,900%
Electrical Equipment, Appliances, and Components	-40%	4%
Motor Vehicles and Parts	-47%	-42%
Other Transportation Equipment	-20%	-13%
Furniture and Related Products	-46%	-20%
Miscellaneous Manufacturing	-24%	60%
Non-Durable Goods Production	-33%	3%
Food, Beverage, and Tobacco Products	-9%	10%
Textile Mills and Textile Products	64%	-47%
Apparel, Leather, and Similar Products	-75%	-46%
Paper Products	-39%	-28%
Printing and Support Activities	-38%	-15%
Petroleum and Coal Products	-10%	70%
Chemical Products	-20%	10%
Plastics and Rubber Products	-33%	-9%

Source: Compiled by the Congressional Research Service from data obtained from the Bureau of Economic Analysis, U.S. Department of Commerce, see http://www.bea.gov/iTable/iTable.cfm?ReqID=5&step=1 for more details.

a.   Value added for an industry measures its contribution to gross domestic product. It is equal to the sum of labor compensation, taxes on production, imports less government subsidies, and gross operating surplus.

Basically, value added represents the difference between an industry's gross output (consisting of sales or receipts and other operating income, commodity taxes, and inventory change) and the cost of its intermediate inputs, including energy, raw materials, semi-finished goods, and services purchased from all sources.

Federal Policy Toward the Manufacturing Sector

Federal support for manufacturing encompasses a number of tax benefits, as well as a variety of spending programs largely intended to promote advanced technology development. The tax benefits are discussed in the next section, while this section provides a brief overview of the programs.

As of April 2011, a total of 10 federal programs targeted assistance to manufacturing firms of all sizes.[6] The assistance involved workforce training, export assistance, business counseling, and technology development, for the most part. Foremost among current programs are the Department of Commerce's (DOC) National Institute of Standard's (NIST) Hollings Manufacturing Extension Partnership program (MEP), which provides technical assistance to small and medium-sized manufacturers to help them become more competitive and productive, and the Advanced Manufacturing Partnership program, which was launched in June 2011 and uses federal funds to leverage the creation of partnerships among businesses, universities, and federal, regional, and state government agencies for the purpose of developing advanced manufacturing technologies. A variety of smaller programs at DOC, the Department of Energy (DOE), the Department of Defense (DOD), and the National Science Foundation (NSF) also support manufacturing, mainly by fostering the development of new manufacturing technologies tailored to the missions of the funding agencies.

There appears to be no comprehensive, reliable estimate of the amount the federal government is spending on programs that support the manufacturing sector. That this is the case is not necessarily a surprise. Generating such an estimate is difficult because such support is delivered through direct and indirect channels. Direct support comes in the form of programs that either target or offer the bulk of their assistance to manufacturing firms. A case in point is MEP, which provides technical assistance to small and medium-sized manufacturing firms only. In general, it is relatively easy to determine the amounts budgeted or spent for programs like that. But such is not the case with federal programs that indirectly support manufacturing. The main difficulty lies in accounting for the value of such support, which can be defined as federal assistance that is not targeted at manufacturing but still benefits a substantial number of manufacturers. A case in point is the research tax credit under Section 41 of the federal tax code: although it is not targeted at manufacturing firms, they are the biggest users of the credit among all sectors. But because the IRS publishes data on claims for the credit by industry and sector, determining the dollar value of the extent to which manufacturing benefits from it can be easily accomplished through the IRS website. A case in point that exemplifies the analytical challenges associated with determining the amount spent on manufacturing through federal programs not targeted at the sector is the programs administered by the Small Business Administration (SBA). While it is safe to assume that numerous small manufacturers have benefited from those programs, it is unclear how much of the agency's budget ($918.8 million in new budget authority for FY2012) has been used to assist such firms.

---

[6] See Nisha Mistry and Joan Byron, *The Federal Role in Supporting Urban Manufacturing*, Brookings Institution, Pratt Center for Community Development, April 2011, p. 34.

Nonetheless, it is possible to get a sense of the magnitude of direct federal non-tax support for manufacturing by parsing President Obama's FY2013 budget proposal for relevant programs. He is asking for $2.2 billion in federal support for research and development (R&D) targeted at advanced manufacturing technology, or 19% more than the amount enacted for FY2012.[7] The funds would go to programs administered by DOC, DOD, DOE, and NSF. Included in the request are $1 billion for a National Network for Manufacturing Innovation to be administered by NIST, $135 million for NIST-sponsored R&D on advanced manufacturing technology, $128 million for MEP, $21 million for NIST's Advanced Manufacturing Technology Consortia Program, $20 million for the NIST Centers for Excellence program, $290 million for DOE's Advanced Manufacturing Office, $149 million for NSF's programs to develop new advanced manufacturing technologies with the involvement of private companies, and $2.8 billion for DOD's Defense Advanced Research Projects Agency, which historically has played a critical role in the development of new products and processes that have had major impacts on the real economy (e.g., integrated circuits, supercomputers, the Internet).

Current Federal Tax Provisions with Significant Benefits for Manufacturing

A useful and necessary point of departure for a summary of current federal tax preferences that offer significant benefits to manufacturing is the definition of a tax preference. Such a preference (which is also known as a tax break, tax benefit, or tax expenditure) is a provision in the federal tax code that grants special tax relief to eligible individual or business taxpayers. The relief is generally intended to promote certain activities, such as the tax credit under section 41 for increasing research expenditures. In some cases, however, it serves the purpose of assisting taxpayers facing certain difficult economic or financial circumstances. The tax relief is considered special because it represents a departure from what the Congressional Budget and Impoundment Control Act of 1974 (P.L. 93-344) refers to as "normal income tax law."

Tax preferences assume any of the following forms: (1) exclusions, exemptions, or deductions, which reduce an eligible taxpayer's taxable income; (2) preferential tax rates, which apply lower rates to part or all of an eligible taxpayer's income; (3) credits, which reduce an eligible taxpayer's tax liability; and (4) tax deferrals, which postpone the recognition of current income for tax purposes or allow deductions in the current tax year that normally are taken in future years.

Tax preferences also produce revenue losses for the U.S. Treasury, relative to the revenue that otherwise would be raised. As a consequence, they are viewed as federal spending (for the intended purposes of the benefits) that is channeled through the tax code. This explains why some refer to tax preferences as tax expenditures. In addition, some contend that permanent tax preferences operate as entitlement programs: in both cases, their benefits are distributed or paid to qualified persons or corporations.[8]

---

[7] See http://www.whitehouse.gov/sites/default/files/microsites/ostp/fy2013omb_innovation.pdf.

[8] U.S. Congress, Senate, Committee on the Budget, *Tax Expenditures: Compendium of Background Material on Individual Provisions*, 111th Cong., 2d sess., S. Prt. 111-58 (Washington: GPO, December 2010), p. 3.

The federal tax code contains numerous provisions granting preferential treatment to companies in an array of industries. In recent years, congressional oversight of business tax benefits generally has been limited to legislation to extend certain temporary benefits that have expired or are about to expire. Permanent business tax benefits have received even less attention.

The business tax preferences from which manufacturing companies tend to derive the most benefit are listed in **Table 2.** Since business tax preferences are not always explicitly intended to benefit manufacturing firms in general, two methods were used to identify the relevant tax provisions. One was the share of overall use of a tax preference (as measured by the aggregate amount claimed on federal tax returns) held by manufacturing firms; the other was the nature of the preference itself, and the extent to which manufacturing firms would be likely to benefit from it, given the nature of their business. Only one of the tax preferences arguably is designed to benefit the manufacturing sector more than others: the deduction for "domestic production activities" income under Section 199 of the federal tax code. Firms in a broad array of industries benefit in varying degrees from the other preferences, but not to the same extent, on the whole, as firms primarily engaged in manufacturing activities.

For each preference shown in the table, the following information is provided:

- a brief description of the tax provision,

- its section in the federal tax code,

- its current status: temporary or permanent,

- its estimated revenue cost in FY2012 for all firms (regardless of industry) that claim it,

- and a summary of its benefits for manufacturing firms.

Several of the provisions in the table are intended to stimulate increased investment in qualified research (Sections 174 and 41), and in equipment and software (Sections 168 and 179), by reducing the cost of capital and boosting cash flow. Tax subsidies for investment in research are considered justified on the grounds that they seek to correct a market failure that leads, in theory, to underinvestment in research by the private sector. But a similar rationale may not apply to tax subsidies for capital investment. Economists who have studied the matter have found no evidence indicating that investment in capital assets like structures and equipment is also prone to some kind of market failure, as firms are able to capture most of the economic returns. Governments typically employ investment tax subsidies as a countercyclical measure during economic downturns. The federal government did so in response to the Great Recession of 2007 to 2009 by extending and increasing the bonus depreciation allowance under Section 168(k) and enhancing the limited expensing allowance under Section 179.

With one exception, the other provisions in the table encourage the following activities: increased domestic investment and expansion by manufacturing firms (Section 199); a larger flow of equity capital to start-up manufacturing firms (Section 1202); greater cash flow among manufacturing firms of all employment sizes (Sections 491, 492, and 168(k)(4)); and increased U.S. exports of manufactured products (Section 861 to 863, 865).

The exception is the first provision shown in the table: the deferral of the active income of controlled foreign corporations (CFCs) under Section 11(b). It is the only tax provision from which U.S.-based manufacturing firms derive significant benefits that encourages them to invest in countries other than the United States. A CFC is any foreign corporation in which U.S.

shareholders own 50% or more of its total voting power or the total value of its stock on any day of a tax year. Under current federal tax law, U.S.-chartered corporations are taxed on their worldwide income. U.S.-based corporations with CFCs are allowed to postpone indefinitely U.S. taxation of their subsidiaries' earnings, as long as the earnings remain in the control of the CFCs and are reinvested abroad. U.S. parent corporations pay federal tax on the earnings only when they are repatriated as intra-firm dividends or certain other income. That tax can be reduced by a credit U.S. corporations may claim for income taxes paid by their foreign subsidiaries to their home countries on the same earnings; the credit is intended to avoid double taxation under U.S. tax law of the same foreign-source income. The option for deferral and the availability of the foreign tax credit give U.S. firms an incentive to establish operations with their own profit centers in countries with relatively low tax rates.

While any U.S.-chartered corporation with CFCs can benefit from deferral, corporations engaged primarily in manufacturing seem to be major beneficiaries. The corporate response to a repatriated earnings provision in the American Jobs Creation Act of 2004 (P.L. 108-357) illustrates this point. Under the provision, U.S. corporations could take a one-time deduction equal to 85% of any increase in their repatriated foreign-source income in either their first tax year beginning on or after the date of enactment or their last tax year beginning before that date. For firms subject to a corporate tax rate of 35%, the deduction lowered the effective rate on the repatriated profits to 5.25%. Credits for foreign taxes paid on the repatriated earnings were reduced by the same amount. In order to claim the deduction, firms had to adopt a domestic investment plan for the repatriated funds. In addition, the deduction was limited to the greater of $500 million or the amount of earnings shown on a firm's books of accounts to be permanently invested outside the United States as of June 30, 2003. According to the conference report on the act, the tax reduction was intended to serve as a temporary economic stimulus measure that would not be extended or enacted again in the future.[9] In a 2008 report on the one-time dividends received deduction, the Internal Revenue Service (IRS) found that manufacturing corporations filed 55% of the returns for the 2004 to 2006 tax years claiming the deduction, and they accounted for 81% of all qualifying dividends.[10] Nearly half of all qualifying dividends were repatriated by firms in the pharmaceutical, electronic, and computer industries.

Table 2. Federal Tax Provisions That Provide Significant Benefits to Manufacturing Firms

Tax Provision	Code Section(s)	Current Status	Total Estimated Revenue Cost for All Users in FY2012	Benefit to Manufacturing Firms
Deferral of active income of controlled foreign corporations	11(d)	Permanent	$14.1 billion	• U.S.-based manufacturing corporations account for a substantial share of the accumulated earnings and profits held by the foreign subsidiaries of U.S. multinational corporations.

[9] U.S. Congress, Conference Committee on the American Jobs Creation Act of 2004, conference report to accompany H.R. 4520, H.Rept. 108-755, 108th Cong., 2nd sess. (Washington: GPO, 2004), p. 314.

[10] Melissa Redmiles, *The One-Time Received Dividend Deduction*, Statistics of Income Bulletin, Washington DC, Spring 2008, available at http://www.irs.gov/pub/irs-soi/08codivdeductbul.pdf.

Tax Provision	Code Section(s)	Current Status	Total Estimated Revenue Cost for All Users in FY2012	Benefit to Manufacturing Firms
				• Provision allows U.S. parent companies to defer U.S. tax on income earned and reinvested by their foreign subsidiaries until the income is repatriated as dividends.
				• Provides an incentive to establish subsidiaries in countries with corporate tax rates lower than U.S. rates.
Research and experimentation tax credit	41	Temporary: expired at the end of 2011	$3.1 billion	• Provision allows firms a tax credit equal to as much as 20% of qualified research spending above a base amount.
				• As a result, it can lower after-tax cost of qualified research, encouraging more investment for that purpose.
				• Manufacturing accounted for 69% of the total value of claims for the credit by corporations in the 2008 and 2009 tax years combined.
Expensing of research and experimental expenditures	174	Permanent	$4.3 billion	• Provision allows firms to deduct spending on qualified research as a current expense, rather than as a capital expense.
				• This treatment lowers the marginal effective tax rate on returns to investment in such research.
				• According to data published by the National Science Foundation, manufacturing firms performed or funded 64% of domestic basic and applied research in 2007.
Accelerated depreciation for certain capital assets, including bonus depreciation in 2012 tax year	168, 168(k), and 179	Section 168: permanent except, for bonus depreciation under Section 168(k), which expires at the end of 2012 Section 179: permanent, though maximum allowance and phase-out threshold can	$31.2 billion	• Section 168 generally allows firms to recover the cost of qualified assets sooner than they can be recovered under the alternative depreciation system in section 167.
				• Section 168(k) establishes a 50% expensing allowance (also known as a bonus depreciation allowance) for qualified property bought and placed in service in 2012; the allowance was 100% in 2011.
				• Section 179 makes it possible for firms to expense a limited amount of the cost of qualified assets placed in service in a tax year.

Tax Provision	Code Section(s)	Current Status	Total Estimated Revenue Cost for All Users in FY2012	Benefit to Manufacturing Firms
		vary from year to year		• Full (or 100%) expensing imposes a 0% marginal effective tax rate on returns to investment in affected assets.
				• Though data on investment by industry in equipment and software are not readily available, it is likely that manufacturing firms account for a major share of total investment in those assets, especially equipment.
Option to claim a refundable accelerated AMT credit in lieu of bonus depreciation allowance	168(k)(4)	Option applies to eligible property acquired after March 31, 2008 and placed in service before January 1, 2013	Not Available	• Provision makes it possible for firms to take a refundable tax credit equal to the lesser of $30 million or 6% of unused AMT credits from tax years before 2006, reduced by (but not below $0) the sum of "bonus depreciation amounts" from all previous tax years.
				• It enables firms in a loss position with longstanding unused AMT credits to increase their cash flow by claiming the optional refundable credit instead of a bonus depreciation allowance that would only boost their net operating loss in the current tax year.
				• Historically, manufacturers have been among the industries most affected by the AMT. In 2008, mining companies accounted for 26.3% of AMT payments, followed by finance/insurance (24.2%), and manufacturing (16.8%).
Deduction for qualified domestic production activities income	199	Permanent	$11.6 billion	• Provision allows firms to deduct 9% of qualified domestic production activities income; the deduction is 6% for activities related to oil and gas production; the deduction cannot exceed a firm's taxable income or 50% of wages linked to those activities.
				• Qualified activities encompass manufacturing, mining, film production, energy, construction, engineering, and architectural services.
				• Deduction lowers the top marginal tax rate on income earned from commercial use of favored property from 35% to 31.85%.
				• In 2008, according to IRS data, manufacturing accounted for 66% of the total value of claims for the domestic production activities deduction by

Tax Provision	Code Section(s)	Current Status	Total Estimated Revenue Cost for All Users in FY2012	Benefit to Manufacturing Firms
				corporations.
Partial exclusion on gains from the sale or exchange of qualified small business stock	1202	Permanent	$0.3 billion	• Provision allows non-corporate taxpayers to exclude from gross income 100% of any gain from the sale or exchange of qualified small business stock acquired after September 27, 2010 and before January 1, 2013; the exclusion reverts to 50% for stock acquired on or after January 1, 2013.
				• To qualify for this treatment, a taxpayer must acquire the stock at original issue and hold it for a minimum of five years.
				• Qualified small business stock must be issued by a C corporation with no more than $50 million in gross assets when the stock is issued.
				• At least 80% of the assets must be used in a qualified trade or business (including manufacturing) during most of the required five-year holding period.
				• Provision is intended to expand access to equity capital by small start-up C corporations that may otherwise have trouble attracting such capital. Large corporations do not benefit from the exclusion.
Inventory accounting: use of the last-in, first-out (LIFO) method	491 and 492	Permanent	$4.3 billion	• Provision allows taxpayers that must maintain inventory records in order to account for the cost of goods sold to exclude any increase in the value of goods they buy or produce from taxable income.
				• LIFO is most beneficial to firms facing rising costs for the goods in their inventories.
				• Research indicates that the vast share of firms that use LIFO for tax purposes are involved in manufacturing.
				• Provision enables taxpayers to reduce the tax burden on the difference between the sales price and cost of inventories.
				• It also creates beneficial tax planning opportunities that do not exist with the first-in, first-out (or FIFO) method of inventory accounting.

Tax Provision	Code Section(s)	Current Status	Total Estimated Revenue Cost for All Users in FY2012	Benefit to Manufacturing Firms
Inventory property sales source rule exception	861 to 863, 865	Permanent	$6.1 billion	• Provision allows U.S. exporters an exception to the rule that income is sourced according to the residence of the seller.
				• Under the exception, inventory that is bought and then re-sold is governed by a rule known as the "title passage" rule.
				• The rule sources income from the sale in the country where the sale occurs.
				• Inventory that is made and sold by the company is treated as having a divided source: half of the income from a sale is sourced in the United States and half in the country where the sale occurs.
				• U.S. companies with excess foreign tax credits may use them to reduce U.S. taxes if they can shift income from U.S. sources to foreign subsidiaries.
				• Companies with excess foreign tax credits can take advantage of the inventory sales source rule exception to increase the amount of their credits that can be applied against their U.S. income tax liability. This has the same effect as exempting from U.S. taxation the income that was sourced in another country as a result of the exception.
				• The source rule exception for inventory sales probably raises the rate of return from investing in exporting.
				• Manufacturers account for two-thirds of U.S. exports of goods and services.

Source: Compiled by the Congressional Research Service from figures provided by the Joint Committee on Taxation and a variety of other sources, including a compendium on tax expenditures released in December 2010 by the Senate Budget Committee. (See http://budget.senate.gov/democratic/index.cfm/files/serve?File_id= 8a03a030-3ba8-4835-a67b-9c4033c03ec4.)

Legislative Initiatives in the 112th Congress to Enhance Existing or Create New Tax Preferences That Benefit Manufacturing Firms

A variety of bills to create new tax preferences that would offer significant benefits for U.S. manufacturing firms, or to extend or enhance existing ones, have been introduced in the 112th

Congress. Summaries of these legislative initiatives are shown in **Table 3**. For each bill, the table describes the preference(s) it would establish and explains how manufacturing firms might benefit from it; provisions in the bills unrelated to tax benefits for manufacturing are not discussed.

Though the policy initiatives to strengthen manufacturing announced by President Obama early in 2012 are not cited in the table, several of the bills would each implement one or more of them. The initiatives were contained in two proposals: his FY2013 budget request and a framework for business tax reform. Several tax proposals in the budget request could have significant short-term benefits for the manufacturing sector, including a one-year extension of the 100% bonus depreciation allowance that was available for qualified assets placed in service in 2011; a 10% tax credit for limited increases from 2011 to 2012 in employer payrolls subject to the Social Security tax; and a doubling of the deduction (from 9% to 18%) for income from domestic production of certain advanced technology products under Section 199. While lacking in details, the proposed business tax reform plan would offer several benefits for manufacturers. First, it would lower of the top corporate income tax rate from 35% to 28%. Second, it would raise the Section 199 deduction for income from the domestic production of manufactured goods to 10.7%. Finally, the expensing allowance for qualified assets under Section 179 would rise to $1 million in a tax year.

Non-Tax Legislation

Legislation to promote the competitiveness and growth of U.S. manufacturing firms through non-tax measures is also being considered in the current Congress. Examples include H.R. 1366, H.R. 1912, H.R. 5727, and S. 751.

H.R. 1366 and S. 751 would mandate the development of a federal strategy to strengthen the U.S. manufacturing sector, but with one notable difference: S. 751 would authorize the Commerce Department to develop the strategy, while H.R. 1366 would assign that responsibility to a commission made up of federal and state government officials and industry representatives.

H.R. 1912 would create an "American Block Grant Program" that would authorize the Commerce Secretary to make grants to governmental entities that in turn would award them to small and medium-sized manufacturers for several purposes, including investing in plant and equipment, producing clean energy products, improving their energy efficiency, and retraining employees to operate new manufacturing technologies. While many manufacturing firms would undoubtedly benefit from the support provided by bills such as these, they are not discussed here, as they lie outside the scope of the report.

H.R. 5737 would improve the competitiveness of U.S. manufacturers by requiring the President to develop and regularly revise a national manufacturing strategy that would pursue several goals, including increasing the number of manufacturing jobs so that they account for 20% of non-agricultural employment. It would also authorize the Commerce Secretary to award grants for the creation of "sectoral technology and innovation centers" to aid small and medium-sized manufacturers; authorize the SBA to offer limited loan guarantees for small manufacturers with firm orders; set funding for MEP at $130 million for each fiscal year from 2013 through 2022, with an adjustment for inflation; extend the research tax credit for three years and increase the rate for the alternative simplified credit for companies that increase their number of qualified full-time manufacturing workers; require that legislation implementing trade agreements between the U.S. government and other countries satisfy certain labor, environmental, and public safety standards; and impose countervailing duties on imports from countries with "fundamentally undervalued" currencies.

Table 3. Legislation in the 112th Congress to Create or Enhance Tax Preferences that Would Benefit U.S.-Based Manufacturing Firms

Bill Number	Tax Provision(s)	Impact on Manufacturing Firms
H.R. 10 and S. 1237	• Would allow manufacturing firms to set up manufacturing reinvestment accounts (MRAs) and deduct (under a new Section 199A) up to $500,000 in cash contributions in a tax year. • Accounts would be managed by designated financial institutions with consolidated assets worth no more than $25 billion. • Would tax distributions from an MRA to pay for qualified reinvestment expenses (QREs) at an effective rate of 15%. • QREs are defined as expenses incurred by an eligible firm for investment in new capital assets or job training and workforce development. • Distributions for other purposes or involving funds deposited more than seven years ago would be subject to regular income tax and a surtax equal to 10% of the amount of the distribution included in a taxpayer's taxable income.	• Could lower the after-tax cost of investing in new plant and equipment and worker training programs for relatively small manufacturing firms. • Would add a layer of complexity to the tax code that may deter eligible firms from taking the deduction and increase the cost of tax compliance for firms that do. • Would create a form of time-limited, tax-free savings for firms that take the deduction. • Would benefit profitable eligible firms planning to expand operations more than other eligible firms.
H.R. 689	• Would permanently extend the research tax credit under Section 41. • Would raise the research credit rate from 20% to 25% for payments for contract research performed by manufacturing firms. • Would increase the deduction for qualified production activities income under Section 199 from 9% to 15% for income from the domestic production of property that was developed mostly through research conducted in the United States.	• Could lead manufacturing firms based anywhere in the world to conduct more qualified research in the United States than they otherwise would. • Could spur an increase in contract research conducted by manufacturing firms located in the United States. • Would give manufacturing companies that develop new technologies in the United States a greater incentive to produce the technologies here. • Would add a layer of complexity to documenting claims for the Section 199.
H.R. 1036[a]	• Would allow U.S.-based corporations with controlled foreign corporations (CFCs) to deduct 85% of any CFC earnings they repatriate in their last tax year before, or first tax year after, the date of enactment. • For corporations subject to the maximum corporate income tax rate of 35%, the enhanced dividends received deduction would reduce the effective rate to 5.25%: (35% x 15%).	• Would allow U.S.-based manufacturing corporations to repatriate any amount of the earnings retained by their foreign subsidiaries at a fraction of the tax rate that normally applies to such a transaction. • They could deduct 85% of the dividends without any requirement

Bill Number	Tax Provision(s)	Impact on Manufacturing Firms
	• The deduction would rise to 100% of repatriated earnings if they are reinvested in a "qualified domestic reinvestment plan." • Such a plan must be approved by the U.S. parent corporation's president (or some comparable official) and board of directors (or comparable body). • The plan must specify that the dividend will be invested in the United States within three years of its repatriation, and that it will be used to fund research and development, "expansion of facilities, proof of concept centers, early stage venture capital investment, or manufacturing start-up costs."	that the repatriated funds be used for a specific purpose. • If the results from a similar deduction that was available under the American Jobs Creation Act of 2004 are any indication, U.S.-based pharmaceutical, electronic, and computer corporations might repatriate tens of billions of dollars under this proposal.
H.R. 3476	• Would extend through 2014 the 100% bonus depreciation allowance that was available from September 9, 2010 through December 31, 2011. • Would also extend through 2014 the option for corporations to exchange any bonus depreciation allowances they could take for a limited amount of their unused AMT credits from tax years before 2006. • Would extend for three years, through 2014, the enhanced expensing allowance under Section 179 that was available in 2010 and 2011. • Would extend through 2014 the 100% exclusion for gains on the sale of qualified small business stock that was acquired in 2011. • Would extend the current research tax credit through 2012, raise the rate for the alternative simplified credit (ASC) from 14% to 20%, and permanently extend the ASC beginning in 2013. Would offer a bonus research tax credit to manufacturers whose domestic production gross receipts exceed 50% of their total production gross receipts; the bonus credit would range in size from two percentage points for shares between 51% and 60% to 10 percentage points for shares greater than 90%. (H.R. 6329 would make the same change in the credit.)	• Would temporarily reduce the cost of capital for investing in new machinery, equipment, and software through the extended generous expensing allowances. • Would temporarily encourage increased equity investment in small start-up manufacturing firms through the extended 100% gains exclusion. • Would encourage increased investment in domestic research that qualifies for the Section 41 credit through the permanent extension of the credit and the increase in the ASC rate. • And would encourage manufacturing companies performing such research to produce in the United States property developed through the research.
H.R. 3495	• Would allow individual and business taxpayers who acquire any of 10 designated manufactured products through retail purchases to claim a new non-refundable tax credit (under Section 30E) equal to the specified percentage of the total amount paid for each product in a tax year during the eligible period for that product. • The specified percentage for each designated product could be no less than 5% and no more than 20%. • The eligible period for a designated product could be no less than five years and no more than 10 years. • A product is considered a designated product if a taxpayer acquires it as a new manufactured product	• Would be likely to stimulate domestic demand for the designated products, though some of the increase may come at the expense of purchases of other products. • Would give U.S.-based manufacturers of designated products an incentive to acquire the capacity to assemble the products in the United States, perhaps by transferring production from offshore operations. • May to boost domestic production

Bill Number	Tax Provision(s)	Impact on Manufacturing Firms
	for her use or lease; it was assembled in the United States; at least 60% of the value of its components and materials originated in the United States; and the Treasury Department has selected the product as one of 10 designated products, in consultation with a commission created under the bill known as the 21st Century American Manufacturing Commission. • In selecting the 10 designated products, the Treasury Department should consider the number of domestic jobs that would be created directly and indirectly through such a selection, and the speed with which they would be created. • The Treasury Secretary would have the authority to specify the credit percentage and eligible period for each of the 10 designated products, in consultation with the Commission. • The credit allowed under the bill would expire 10 years after the date of enactment	of affected components and materials. • Would add a layer of complexity to the tax code and increase the cost of compliance for taxpayers claiming the credit and firms that manufacture designated products.
H.R. 5727	• Would extend the research tax credit through the end of 2016. • Would modify the ASC to increase the 14% rate by up to six percentage points for increases in a taxpayer's qualified full-time equivalent (FTE) "manufacturing employment." • The ASC rate would rise by one percentage point for every 2% rise in a taxpayer's FTE during the previous five tax years. • Any increase in the research credit in a tax year would be capped at amount equal to $5,000 multiplied by the number of qualified FTE employees. • A manufacturing employee is defined as an employee engaged in full-time work in qualified production activities under Section 199(c), except for the extraction of oil and minerals and agriculture.	• Would give manufacturers based anywhere in the world that conduct research that qualifies for the Section 41 credit an incentive to invest in domestic production.
H.R. 6240	• Would extend the research credit through 2016 and increase the rate for the ASC to 25%. • Would extend the 100% bonus depreciation allowance under Section 168(k) that was available in 2011 through 2013. • Would extend through 2012 the $500,000 expending allowance and $2 million phaseout threshold under Section 179 that were available in 2010 and 2011. • Would reduce the maximum corporate tax rate to 25% for the 2013 tax year. • Would extend by one year, through 2013, the Bush-era tax cuts for individuals.	• Would reduce the after-tax cost of qualified research. • Would lower the marginal effective tax rate on the returns from investments in assets eligible for bonus depreciation made in 2012 and 2013 to zero. • Would cut by 10 percentage points the top corporate tax rate for 2013, increasing cash flow and the after-tax returns on certain previous investments. • Would prevent in 2013 an increase in the taxation of the profits earned by businesses organized as passthrough entities.

Bill Number	Tax Provision(s)	Impact on Manufacturing Firms
S. 256	• Would allow an accredited investor, an investor network, or an investor fund to claim a new non-refundable tax credit (under Section 30E) equal to 25% of equity investments in qualified domestic corporations or partnerships. • The total credit available to all eligible businesses would be capped at $500 million for the period from FY2011 to FY2013. • The credit would be part of the general business credit under Section 38 and thus subject to its limitations. • A qualified investor must acquire the equity or capital interest at its original issue. • To qualify for the credit, the investment must be made in a domestic corporation or partnership headquartered in the United States. In addition, it must engage in a trade or business related to advanced materials, nanotechnology, precision manufacturing, aerospace, defense, biotechnology and pharmaceuticals, electronics, computer technology (including software), semiconductors, clean energy technology, forest products, agriculture, information and communication technologies, life and medical sciences, marine technology, and transportation. Moreover, the corporation or partnership has to be less than five years old and cannot have more than 99 full-time equivalent employees (more than half of whom are performing their services in the United States) on the date of an equity investment. • The equity investments eligible for the credit would be capped at $10 million for a single qualified business in its lifetime; $2 million for a single qualified business in a tax year; and $1 million for a single qualified investor in a tax year.	• Would be likely to increase access to needed capital for some small start-up firms. • Unlike the gains exclusion under Section 1202 for qualified business stock, there would be no required holding period for the equity eligible for the credit. • Would add a layer of complexity to the tax code that would have implications for the cost of compliance and information reporting for qualified investors and the firms they invest in, as well as the cost to the Internal Revenue Service of enforcing tax law.
S. 825	• Would permanently extend the research credit under Section 41, retaining only the alternative simplified credit and increasing its rate from 14% to 20%. • Would allow domestic manufacturers that derive more than 50% of their total production income from domestic production to claim a bonus credit under Section 41; the increase in the bonus credit would range from two percentage points for shares between 51% and 60% to 10 percentage points for shares greater than 90%. • Would make the Section 41 credit refundable for firms with an average of 500 or fewer employees in the current tax year.	• Might allow more manufacturing firms to benefit from the Section 41 credit. • Would encourage manufacturers conducting qualified research in the United States to invest more in domestic production and hire more U.S. workers.
S. 2237	• Would allow employers that increase their total payroll subject to the Social Security tax in 2012 relative their payroll in 2011 to claim a non-refundable credit equal to 10% of the excess, which would be capped at $5 million for a single taxpayer, making the	• Would encourage manufacturing firms to expand their payroll in 2012 through wage increases and new hiring by reducing the after-tax cost of doing so.

Bill Number	Tax Provision(s)	Impact on Manufacturing Firms
	maximum credit per taxpayer $500,000.	• Would stimulate demand for capital equipment, boosting the output of domestic makers of the equipment.
	• Would extend through 2012 the 100% bonus depreciation allowance that was available for qualified assets acquired and placed in service in 2011.	
	• Would also extend through 2012 the option for corporations to exchange any bonus depreciation allowances they could take that year for a portion of any of their unused AMT credits from tax years before 2006.	• Would reduce the cost of capital and increase cash flow for manufacturers acquiring assets eligible for full expensing in 2012.
S. 3217/ H.R. 5893	• Would permanently exempt from taxation any capital gains on the sale or exchange of small business stock under Section 1202.	• Small startup manufacturing firms would among the main beneficiaries of the two tax benefits.
	• Would create a limited refundable research tax credit for relatively young small businesses.	

Source: Congressional Research Service

a. At least 10 other bills would reinstate a dividends received deduction for repatriated foreign earnings: H.R. 937, H.R. 1834, H.R. 2862, H.R. 3400, H.R. 3448, H.R. 3460, S. 727, S. 1671, S. 1837, and S. 2091. Some are more generous than the deduction proposed in H.R. 1036; others less so. Some would impose stringent requirements on the use of the repatriated funds as a condition of claiming the enhanced dividends received deduction.

Current Policy Debate Over Whether To Increase Federal Support for the Manufacturing Sector

Today's policy debate over the need for more federal support for manufacturing has a precedent: the debate over industrial policy that at times dominated U.S. economic policy discussions in the first half of the 1980s. In both cases, a primary concern was (and is) the long-term economic consequences of a shrinking domestic manufacturing base in the face of growing foreign competition in global markets for advanced technology products.

In the 1970s and early 1980s, U.S.-based companies in an broad expanse of industries (e.g., steel, automobiles, textiles, footwear, consumer electronics, semiconductors, and machine tools) experienced intensifying and adaptive competition from companies based in Japan, South Korea, France, Canada, Italy, West Germany, and Great Britain. As a result, major U.S. companies lost market share at home and abroad, leading to declines in revenue, profits, and company budgets for critical investments like R&D. Of particular concern to many lawmakers and analysts at the time was the rising competitiveness of European and Japanese companies in commercial markets for advanced technologies in aerospace, telecommunications, computer software, electronics, semiconductors, and the equipment used to produce integrated circuits. Their gains in market share worldwide gave rise to bipartisan support in Congress for several new federal initiatives to bolster the competitiveness of U.S. producers of these products, including the research tax credit that was enacted in 1981. These initiatives were predicated on the belief that some industries were more valuable or mattered more than others to sustained growth in U.S. output of goods and services and income per capita. Such a view implied that the federal government should adopt whatever policy measures are needed to uphold and strengthen the competitiveness of American-based companies in high-technology industries. The industries targeted for federal assistance in the 1980s were all part of the manufacturing sector.

Fast forward to the present. Manufacturing accounts for smaller shares of GDP and employment and was hit hard by the severe recession that began in December 2007 and ended in June 2009. The sector again is the focus of a lively policy debate. This time the main concern is not so much the potential long-term economic losses from intensified foreign competition, but the potential long-term economic gains that might arise from the federal government taking a strategic approach to fostering the growth of U.S. manufacturing companies, especially those that develop and produce domestically advanced technology products like smartphones, the latest generation of video games, and the sophisticated electronic components that enable these products to perform the way they do.

So as Congress debates the merits of proposals to boost federal support for manufacturing, it may find it useful to consider the main arguments for and against targeted federal support for the manufacturing sector and their implications for public policy.

Arguments Made for Special Assistance

Proponents of special assistance for manufacturing offer several arguments in support of their position. The arguments relate to the contribution of manufactured products to U.S. exports, the wages and benefits available in the manufacturing sector, the role of manufacturing in technological innovation, the links between manufacturing and the development and production of so-called green technologies, and policies supporting manufacturing adopted by other countries.

First, proponents point out that most economists think the United States would be better off relying less on consumption and imports financed by foreign borrowing to grow its economy and relying more on domestic production of goods and exports. Manufactured products (mainly chemicals, transportation equipment, computers and other electronic products, and machinery) account for around 65% of U.S. exports of goods and 73% of U.S imports of goods,[11] and trade in goods is responsible for about 130% of the U.S. trade deficit. As proponents like to emphasize, these shares demonstrate that manufacturing would play a leading role in any sensible policy option for reducing the U.S. trade deficit. Therefore, say proponents, the federal government should launch renewed efforts to dismantle the remaining foreign barriers to exports of U.S. manufactured products and persuade major exporting nations like China to adopt more flexible exchange rate regimes. They also call for the adoption of federal policies to bolster the competitiveness of U.S. manufacturers through coordinated investments in workforce development, equipment, software, and R&D.

Second, proponents point out that wages and benefits provided by manufacturing firms are larger, on average, than wages and benefits provided in other non-agricultural industries, as shown in **Figure 1**, though the gap has been shrinking over time. For instance, between 2005 and 2010, according to data reported by the Bureau of Labor Statistics, average weekly earnings in manufacturing were 21% greater than average weekly earnings in all private non-agricultural

---

[11] These figures represent the average shares for the first three months of both 2011 and 2012 and are based on the latest report by the U.S. Bureau of the Census on U.S. international trade in goods and services. See http://www.census.gov/foreign-trade/Press-Release/2012pr/03/ft900.pdf.

industries. And a recent study by Mark Price of the Keystone Research Center, which controlled for the key factors affecting wages such as the nature of the job and characteristics of workers, found that manufacturing workers earned 8.4% more each week than non-manufacturing workers from 2008 to 2010.[12] Not all non-manufacturing industries pay less than the average wage in manufacturing. The ones that do pay more, according to Price's research findings, such as mining, utilities, telecommunications, finance, insurance, professional and technical services, hospitals, and public administration, accounted for only 21% of total non-manufacturing workers. Price also found that low-wage workers benefitted the most from manufacturing jobs and high-wage workers benefitted the least, suggesting that manufacturing has a significant potential to lower wage gaps among workers. Proponents also note that manufacturing jobs are more likely to provide fringe benefits than non-manufacturing jobs, and that a higher share of manufacturing workers (48%) have no formal education beyond a high-school diploma than do non-manufacturing workers (37%).[13] These considerations, proponents say, demonstrate that added federal support for manufacturing could contribute to greater middle-income job opportunities and less income inequality among domestic workers.

Third, proponents cite the critical links between manufacturing and technological innovation as yet another reason why federal policy should offer special support for manufacturing firms. According to data reported by the National Science Foundation (NSF), manufacturing firms as a whole were responsible for 70% of the business R&D conducted in the United States and paid for by companies in 2009,[14] and they employed 34% more research scientists and engineers per 1,000 employees than did non-manufacturing industries in 2007.[15] Since technological innovation is thought to be the principal engine of long-term growth in living standards and the economy, proponents maintain that the federal government should adopt policies that encourage U.S.-based multinational manufacturers to conduct more of their R&D in the United States than they already do. Commerce Department data show that U.S.-based multinational companies in all lines of business conducted an average of 84% of their R&D in U.S. facilities in 2007 and 2008.[16] But this share has been declining in recent years, as these companies have transferred some of their R&D operations to Asia in response to growing markets, ample supplies of well-educated and well-trained researchers and engineers willing to work at salaries below what is paid for similar work in the United States, and generous government subsidies.

In addition, proponents say the manufacturing sector makes a "disproportionately large" contribution to the development and production of goods and services with clear environmental benefits. A recent report by the Brookings Institution estimated that 26% of the 2.7 million jobs in the "clean economy" are in the manufacturing sector, even though those jobs represent only 9% of private-sector jobs.[17] Proponents go on to note that a number of critical green technologies and

[12] Susan Helper, Timothy Krueger, and Howard Wial, *Why Does Manufacturing Matter? Which Manufacturing Matters?*, Metropolitan Policy Program, Brookings Institution, February 2012, p. 4.

[13] Ibid., p. 5.

[14] Raymond M. Wolfe, *Business R&D Performed in the United States Cost $291 Billion in 2008 and $282 Billion in 2009*, National Science Foundation, National Center for Science and Engineering Statistics, InfoBrief, NSF-12-309 (Arlington, VA: March 2012), p. 2.

[15] National Science Foundation, National Center for Science and Engineering Statistics, *Research and Development in Industry: 2006-07*, detailed statistical tables, NSF 11-301 (Arlington, VA: June 2011), Table 68.

[16] Kevin B. Barefoot and Raymond J. Mataloni, Jr., "U.S. Multinational Companies: Operations in the United States and Abroad in 2008," in *Survey of Current Business*, Department of Commerce, Bureau of Economic Analysis, vol. 90, no. 8, August 2010, Tables 15, 16.1, and 16.2 (pp. 221-223).

[17] Helper, Krueger, and Wial, *Why Does Manufacturing Matter?* p. 14.

products are made by manufacturing firms, including electric vehicles, water-efficient products, energy-efficient appliances, and environmentally friendly chemical products. So in their view, a competitive, growing manufacturing sector is needed to provide the United States with the workforce skills, engineering talent, and innovative capability required to meet the twin technological challenges of producing more clean energy and reducing the consumption of energy made from fossil fuels. Proponents say that special federal assistance might make that happen.

Yet another argument made in support of federal policies to assist manufacturing is that many other countries do so, some with notable success.[18] According to proponents, the exemplar is Germany. They maintain that the federal government would do well to emulate German policy toward manufacturing, the constraints imposed by the current U.S. political climate notwithstanding. Compared to the United States, Germany has achieved better outcomes in manufacturing in recent years, as exemplified by higher wages, a slower rate of job loss, and large trade surpluses. Research indicates that these results are due in part to public policies that have fostered the emergence of dense R&D networks that cut across industry boundaries, supported a system of continuous vocational training tied to industry needs, promoted stable access to finance for small and mid-sized German companies, and encouraged the rise of a collaborative system involving unions and companies for making important decisions on issues not subject to collective bargaining. In view of proponents, the German example proves that public policy can address the basic challenges facing the manufacturing sector in ways that allow a country to achieve such critical policy objectives as relatively high wages, increased technological innovation, greater trade surpluses, improved environmental protection, and greater energy conservation.[19]

It should be pointed out that not all proponents call for special assistance to any and all firms classified as manufacturing, regardless of their size and the impact of their performance on other firms and consumers. Some argue that federal policymakers should take into account the differences in performance and external benefits among industries involved in goods production so they can devise policies that effectively encourage the migration of workers to current and future high-growth industries, remedy market failures that permit relatively inefficient firms to remain in business, and help firms with relatively low productivity to raise it.[20] To provide special assistance to manufacturing firms that are hopelessly uncompetitive, say these proponents, would end up wasting taxpayer money. Others tweak this line of reasoning by contending that the federal government and companies operating in the United States should make needed changes in their investment strategies to restore the "ability of enterprises to develop and manufacture high-technology products in America.[21]" Still others contend that government policy should provide special assistance to small and medium-sized manufacturers only since they serve as "key drivers of employment and technology growth" but lag behind large firms in adopting "new technologies that would make them more productive.[22]" Proponents of this approach also maintain that small

---

[18] For an assessment of the support for manufacturing offered by Australia, Canada, Germany, Japan, Spain, and the United Kingdom, see Information Technology & Innovation Foundation, *International Benchmarking of Countries' Policies and Programs Supporting SME Manufacturers* (Washington: September 2011). Available at http://www.itif.org/publications/international-benchmarking-countries%E2%80%99-policies-and-programs-supporting-sme-manufacturer.

[19] Helper, Krueger, and Wial, *Why Manufacturing Matters*, p.28.

[20] Ibid., p. 15.

[21] Gary P. Pisano and Willy C. Shih, " Restoring American Competitiveness," *Harvard Business Review*, July-August 2009, p. 114.

[22] Stephen Ezell, "Revitalizing U.S. Manufacturing," *Issues in Science and Technology*, Winter 2012, available at (continued...)

---

and medium-sized manufacturers deserve targeted assistance because they face special difficulties in gaining needed public information and advisory services and play "critical roles" in supporting the competitiveness of a country's large manufacturers.

Arguments Made Against Special Assistance

Not everyone agrees special government assistance for manufacturing is the key to laying a solid foundation for sustained economic growth with relatively high wages for lower- and middle-class workers. In fact, some analysts and lawmakers question the need for such support. Their doubts rest, in part, on several arguments that critics of special assistance for manufacturing have been making at least since the early 1980s. The arguments concern the lack of any market failures linked to manufacturing, the seemingly irreversible shrinkage in the contributions of the manufacturing sector to job creation and GDP over the past 50 years or so, and the untapped potential for growth in U.S. exports of services in which the United States may have a comparative advantage.

One argument rests on the absence of market failures in manufacturing. In general, a market failure is a condition that prevents or hinders the emergence of an efficient allocation of resources within a particular market, such as the market for health insurance or passenger cars. Most economists would agree that government intervention is justified when the workings of the free market do not lead to efficient or equitable outcomes in particular markets. For instance, if competition in a market is limited, antitrust laws can be used to lessen any welfare loss by curtailing the market power of the leading sellers. The main market failures involve the following conditions: public goods, externalities (positive and negative), a lack of competition, the absence of a market, incomplete and asymmetric information, and the so-called principal-agent dilemma.

In the case of manufacturing, such a view implies that federal support is warranted only if a market failure is causing inefficient resource allocations within the sector, such as sub-optimal investment in R&D or capital assets like structures and equipment. Yet some economists and other analysts would argue that there is no evidence of such a problem that is peculiar to the sector as a whole. Though they recognize there is a market failure in the form of positive externalities associated with investments in R&D that broadly affects manufacturing, they point out that these externalities have the potential to affect R&D investments across all sectors. As these critics of targeted government assistance for manufacturing note, some non-manufacturing firms, such as those involved in software development, also invest substantial amounts in R&D and thus are just as likely as manufacturing firms to underinvest in R&D relative to its overall social benefits. In their view, the preferred approach to correcting such a market failure is to do what the federal government already does: provide subsidies for R&D investment that firms in all lines of business could benefit from if they qualify.

The same point can be made about the clustering of businesses from the same industry in specific geographic areas. According to critics, there is reason to believe that clusters of manufacturing firms can be more productive than individual ones. As a result, when an investor builds a plant in an area where such clustering exists, some of the returns on investment are likely to accrue to other firms in the area. These leakages could justify government subsidies or tax benefits for the

---

(...continued)

http://www.issues.org/28.2/ezell.html.

investor. But critics say that research on the economic benefits of clustering has failed to uncover such effects on a large scale.[23] They also point out that whatever external benefits arise from clustering are likely to apply in industries outside manufacturing as well, such as software development, insurance, and entertainment.

A similar objection applies to learning by doing as a source of market failure, say some critics. They note there is no evidence that the process, which encompasses the time, analysis, and adjustments required to make a new production process work efficiently, tends to prevent companies developing new production methods from reaping most of the eventual returns from those investments. If the opposite were true, then government subsidies or tax benefits might be needed to ensure that private firms continue to invest in process innovations in optimal or near-optimal amounts. But such is not the case, say critics. To prove their point, they cite a study of the U.S. semiconductor industry that found that while learning by doing was a substantial cost of investing in new production methods, most of the rewards went to the companies making the initial investments.[24]

Nor is it the case, in the view of critics, that the external benefits associated with national defense spending justify special treatment for all manufacturers. They contend that not all such firms are equally critical to a war effort. In addition, they say there is no reason why the existing U.S. production base for defense goods, supplemented by military supply arrangements with allies, would necessarily be incapable of providing adequate supplies of weapons and other needed materials during a war.[25]

Critics argue that the appropriate policy response to any underinvestment caused by positive externalities is a subsidy intended to boost investment. Federal policy does this in the case of R&D investment by funding research that most companies are loath to undertake on their own and providing tax subsidies for private-sector spending on qualified research. In the view of critics, to channel financial support to manufacturing in the absence of market failures would be to distort the allocation of economic resources among sectors, leading to lower levels of social welfare.

A second argument raised against special assistance for manufacturing concerns job creation. Some critics say it would be misguided for the federal government to direct special assistance at manufacturing in the expectation that it would trigger large employment gains over time. Domestic employment in the sector has been gradually shrinking (with a few temporary upturns) since 1979 and now accounts for 9% of total U.S. non-farm employment. In the view of critics, most of the factory jobs lost over the past three decades are gone forever. Moreover, even if all U.S. multinational companies were to stop outsourcing production and imports of manufactured products were denied entry into the United States, they maintain that growth in domestic manufacturing employment would be likely to continue to fall relative to other sectors for a simple reason: Americans are spending less of their disposable incomes on goods and more on services, a trend that has been gaining momentum since the late 1970s. Critics also note that the main cause of the sluggish U.S. job growth since the end of the Great Recession in June 2009 has been persistently weak aggregate demand. Thus, increasing assistance to manufacturing firms would do little to boost job creation in the short run, since it would have little effect on overall

---

[23] Christina D. Romer, "Do Manufacturers Need Special Treatment," *New York Times*, February 4, 2012.

[24] Ibid.

[25] Ibid.

demand. A more cost-effective policy option for spurring faster job creation, say critics, would be to enact measures that increase total spending right away, such as tax cuts for low- and middle-income households, increased aid to state and local governments, or large public investments in infrastructure modernization and expansion.

Finally, critics say the U.S. economy would probably benefit more in the short run from government efforts to dismantle foreign barriers to U.S. exports of services than from new programs to bolster the competitiveness of U.S. manufacturers. They say the United States has a greater comparative advantage in highly skilled services such as engineering, law, finance, and architecture than in products made with the use of low-skilled workers (e.g., apparel, wood products, processed food). In addition, service industries, broadly defined, employ about 70% of American non-farm workers, and the United States is the leading exporter of services in the world. Nonetheless, according to critics, there is considerable untapped potential for expanding the U.S. share. Current service exports come from a small percentage of U.S. companies, and there is a boom in infrastructure development in faster-growing economies like China, India, and Brazil. According to an estimate by J. Bradford Jensen, an economist with the Petersen Institute for International Economics, the United States has the potential to more than double its current service exports if existing barriers overseas were removed, creating an additional $800 billion in tradable business services like law and engineering.[26] Such an increase would support or create nearly three million U.S. jobs, according to Jensen, and those jobs would be likely to pay higher wages than manufacturing jobs, on average. Given these possible gains, critics argue that the federal government should boost its efforts to press other governments to open up their service markets to U.S. companies. It should also, in their view, loosen U.S. immigration controls and work with other countries to relax theirs; such controls can restrain the growth of service exports by hindering the free movement of service workers across national borders.

Implications of the Arguments for Federal Policy

The pro and con arguments related to the federal role in the manufacturing sector have implications for how federal policy should respond to the current challenges facing the sector. The main ones are considered below.

First of all, the arguments and the evidence cited in support of them suggest there is no clear and indisputable economic rationale for providing special federal support for the manufacturing sector. Goods production as an economic activity seems generally free of market failures. Some try to make a convincing case to the contrary based on manufacturing's central role in technological innovation in the private sector, the positive external benefits associated with private-sector R&D investment, and the "direct linkages" between manufacturing and well-paying service jobs throughout the economy. But such an argument may lose some of its appeal and plausibility when one considers the steps the federal government has taken since the 1950s to lift business R&D investment to levels thought to be more in line with the economic returns to innovation. These steps include a tax credit and an expensing allowance for expenditures on qualified research. Since eligibility for these tax benefits depends critically on the nature of the research a firm conducts or finances, they have the significant advantage, relative to an R&D tax subsidy aimed at manufacturers only, of stimulating increased investment in innovative activity across all sectors, not just in manufacturing. The market failure inherent in such investment in

---

[26] Catherine Rampell, "Some Urge U.S. to Focus on Selling Its skills Overseas," *New York Times*, April 10, 2012.

theory affects firms in all lines of business, not just manufacturing; so policy measures to remedy the failure arguably should be targeted at all sectors.

In addition, it is unlikely that special aid for manufacturing would spark a significant rise in job creation in the current economy. The sector's contribution to overall employment has been declining for more than three decades and now stands at 9% of U.S. non-farm employment. And the U.S. Department of Labor reports that private-sector payroll employment rose by 4.267 million from its most recent low in February 2010 to May 2012; manufacturing contributed 495,000 jobs to that gain, or 11.6%. In an economy marked by lingering high unemployment sustained by insufficient aggregate demand, increased support for manufacturing may have less bang for the buck in its impact on job creation than policy options intended to deliver a quick, sizable stimulus to aggregate demand. Examples include increases in federal spending on infrastructure, transfers of federal funds to state and local governments, or tax cuts for households. In the long run, it is economic growth that underpins and drives job creation.

The arguments also indicate that some of the proposals to harness federal policy to the goal of bolstering the competitiveness of U.S. manufacturers would have similar benefits for other sectors, augmenting the overall return on federal spending for that purpose. Some proponents of a federal manufacturing policy say it should address four major issues: increased R&D support, greater investment in worker training, improved access to investment capital, and new mechanisms for creating and sharing productivity improvements and other innovations among competing firms. There is no reason why firms in other industries could or would not benefit from similar policies. So rather than focusing on manufacturing, Congress may wish to consider cost-effective policy options for providing more R&D support, improving worker training to reduce mismatches between employer skill needs and the skill sets of workers, expanding access to credit for small- and medium-sized companies, and encouraging the growth of industry-specific networks that could offer a range of collaborative services for the mutual benefit of individual firms that would apply to all sectors.

Finally, though this issue is not explicitly addressed in any of the pro and con arguments considered earlier, Congress may want to look at the advantages and disadvantages of using tax incentives as a tool for achieving any policy objectives it may set for manufacturing industries. Tax incentives require no annual appropriations to enable them to have their intended effect. But they can operate like hidden entitlements that can impose significant compliance burdens on companies and enforcement costs on the IRS, which has been facing growing pressure from Congress in the past few years to do more with less. By contrast, spending programs tend to be more transparent and open to congressional oversight. The comparative advantages of spending programs (including credit guarantees) and tax incentives may come under greater scrutiny as Congress debates options for achieving long-term reductions in budget deficits and federal debt, including fundamental tax reform, in coming months. This issue has already surfaced in some proposals for Congress to expand federal support for manufacturing by enacting measure that involve no tax benefits. One such proposal calls for the following initiatives:

- establishing a National Laboratory for Advanced Manufacturing to undertake engineering research on early-stage applications that might be useful in a variety of manufacturing processes;

- offering competitive grants to organized groups of manufacturers and related institutions to help them to collectively solve common problems, such as worker training;

- expanding and modernizing the MEP to provide more assistance to small and medium-sized firms in designing new products, finding new markets, and distributing and marketing products; and

- providing competitive grants to companies that engage in high-wage production in the United States. [27]

Author Contact Information

Gary Guenther
Analyst in Public Finance
gguenther@crs.loc.gov, 7-7742

---

[27] Susan Helper and Howard Wial, *Strengthening American Manufacturing : A New Federal Approach*, Brookings Institution, Metropolitan Policy Program (Washington: September 27, 2010). Available at http://www.brookings.edu/~/media/research/files/papers/2010/9/27%20great%20lakes/0927_great_lakes_manufacturing.pdf.
